contents

Please note that Australian cup and
spoon measurements are metric.
A conversion chart appears on page 62.

dark chocolate mud cake

250g butter, chopped
150g dark eating chocolate, chopped coarsely
2 cups (440g) white sugar
1 cup (250ml) hot water
⅓ cup (80ml) whisky
1 tablespoon instant coffee granules
1½ cups (225g) plain flour
¼ cup (35g) self-raising flour
¼ cup (25g) cocoa powder
2 eggs, beaten lightly

1 Preheat oven to 160°C/140°C fan-forced. Grease 23cm-square slab pan; line base and sides with baking paper, extending paper 5cm above sides.
2 Combine butter, chocolate, sugar, the water, whisky and coffee in medium saucepan; stir over low heat until mixture is smooth, cool. Stir in sifted flours and cocoa then egg.
3 Pour mixture into pan; bake about 1¼ hours. Stand 10 minutes then turn, top-side up, onto wire rack to cool. Cut into nine pieces; serve dusted with sifted icing sugar, if desired.

preparation time 10 minutes (plus cooling time)
cooking time 1 hour 20 minutes
serves 9

white chocolate mud cake

250g butter, chopped
180g white eating chocolate,
  chopped coarsely
1½ cups (330g) caster sugar
¾ cup (180ml) milk
1½ cups (225g) plain flour
½ cup (75g) self-raising flour
½ teaspoon vanilla extract
2 eggs, beaten lightly
white chocolate ganache
½ cup (125ml) thickened cream
360g white eating chocolate,
  chopped finely
chocolate curls
1⅓ cups (200g) dark chocolate
  Melts, melted
1⅓ cups (200g) white chocolate
  Melts, melted
1⅓ cups (200g) milk chocolate
  Melts, melted

1 Preheat oven to 160°C/140°C fan-forced. Grease deep 20cm-round cake pan; line base and side with baking paper.

2 Combine butter, chocolate, sugar and milk in medium saucepan; stir over low heat until melted. Transfer mixture to large bowl; cool 15 minutes.

3 Stir in sifted flours, extract and egg; pour into pan. Bake about 1 hour 40 minutes; cool cake in pan.

4 Meanwhile, make white chocolate ganache and chocolate curls.

5 Turn cake, top-side up, onto serving plate. Spread ganache all over cake; top with chocolate curls.

white chocolate ganache Bring cream to the boil in small saucepan; pour over chocolate in medium bowl, stir with wooden spoon until chocolate melts. Cover bowl; refrigerate, stirring occasionally, about 30 minutes or until spreadable.

chocolate curls Spread dark, white and milk chocolate separately on marble slab or bench top. When chocolate is almost set, drag ice-cream scoop over surface of chocolate to make curls. Set chocolate can be scraped up, re-melted and used again.

preparation time 50 minutes
(plus cooling and refrigeration time)
cooking time 1 hour 45 minutes
serves 12

chocolate chip apricot cake

1 cup (150g) coarsely chopped dried apricots
1 cup (250ml) apricot nectar
125g butter, softened
⅔ cup (150g) raw sugar
2 eggs, separated
1½ cups (120g) desiccated coconut
1½ cups (225g) self-raising flour
½ cup (95g) dark choc Bits

1 Preheat oven to 180°C/160°C fan-forced. Grease deep 20cm-round cake pan; line base with baking paper.
2 Combine apricots and nectar in medium bowl; stand 1 hour.
3 Beat butter and sugar in small bowl with electric mixer until light and fluffy. Add egg yolks, beat until combined.
4 Transfer mixture to large bowl; stir in coconut then half the sifted flour and half the apricot mixture. Stir in remaining flour, remaining apricot mixture then choc Bits.
5 Beat egg whites in small bowl with electric mixer until soft peaks form; fold into apricot mixture.
6 Spread mixture into pan; bake about 1¼ hours. Stand cake 5 minutes then turn, top-side up, onto wire rack to cool.
7 Serve cake dusted with sifted icing sugar, if desired.

preparation time 15 minutes (plus standing and cooling time)
cooking time 1 hour 15 minutes
serves 8
note Cake will keep in an airtight container for up to three days.

dark chocolate Drambuie fruit cake

2⅓ cups (375g) sultanas
2¼ cups (335g) raisins,
  chopped coarsely
1⅔ cups (270g) dried currants
1½ cups (250g) prunes,
  seeded, chopped coarsely
1½ cups (210g) dried dates,
  seeded, chopped coarsely
⅔ cup (140g) red glacé
  cherries, quartered
1⅓ cups (330ml) Drambuie
⅓ cup (120g) honey
¾ cup (120g) mixed peel
1 tablespoon finely grated
  lemon rind
250g butter, softened
1½ cups (330g) firmly packed
  dark brown sugar
6 eggs
90g dark eating chocolate,
  coarsely grated
1¼ cups (150g) pecans,
  chopped coarsely
2 cups (300g) plain flour
1 cup (150g) self-raising flour
¼ cup (25g) cocoa powder

1 Combine fruit, 1 cup of the Drambuie, honey, peel and rind in large bowl. Cover tightly with plastic wrap; store in a cool, dark place overnight or up to a week, stirring every day.

2 On the day of baking, preheat oven to 120°C/100°C fan-forced. Grease six-hole (¾-cup/180ml) texas muffin pan. Grease deep 22cm-round cake pan; line base and side with four thicknesses of baking paper, extending paper 5cm above edge.

3 Beat butter and sugar with electric mixer until just combined. Add eggs, beating until combined between additions. Stir into fruit mixture with chocolate and nuts. Stir in sifted dry ingredients, in two batches.

4 Fill each hole of the muffin pan, level to the top, with mixture; spread remaining mixture into cake pan. Decorate tops with extra pecans and glacé cherries, if desired.

5 Bake muffins 1½ hours (cake can stand while muffins are baking). Brush hot muffins with some of the remaining Drambuie; cover with foil, cool in pan.

6 Increase oven temperature to 150°C/130°C fan-forced. Bake large cake about 3 hours. Brush hot cake with remaining Drambuie; cover hot cake with foil; cool in pan overnight.

preparation time 50 minutes
(plus standing and cooling time)
cooking time 4 hours 30 minutes
serves 36
note Cake can be made up to three months ahead; store in an airtight container in the refrigerator, or freeze for up to 12 months.

hazelnut chocolate cake

⅓ cup (35g) cocoa powder
⅓ cup (80ml) hot water
150g dark eating chocolate, melted
150g butter, melted
1⅓ cups (295g) firmly packed brown sugar
1 cup (100g) hazelnut meal
4 eggs, separated
1 tablespoon cocoa powder, extra

1 Preheat oven to 180°C/160°C fan-forced. Grease deep 19cm-square cake pan; line base and sides with baking paper.
2 Blend cocoa with the water in large bowl until smooth. Stir in chocolate, butter, sugar, hazelnut meal and egg yolks.
3 Beat egg whites in small bowl with electric mixer until soft peaks form; fold into chocolate mixture in two batches.
4 Pour mixture into pan; bake about 1 hour or until firm. Stand cake 15 minutes; turn, top-side up, onto wire rack to cool. Dust with sifted extra cocoa to serve.

preparation time 20 minutes (plus standing and cooling time)
cooking time 1 hour
serves 9
notes Hazelnut meal replaces the flour in this recipe.
This cake can be made up to four days ahead; keep, covered, in the refrigerator. Cake can also be frozen for up to three months.

family chocolate cake

2 cups (500ml) water
3 cups (660g) caster sugar
250g butter, chopped
⅓ cup (35g) cocoa powder
1 teaspoon bicarbonate
  of soda
3 cups (450g) self-raising flour
4 eggs, beaten lightly
fudge frosting
90g butter
⅓ cup (80ml) water
½ cup (110g) caster sugar
1½ cups (240g) icing sugar
⅓ cup (35g) cocoa powder

1 Preheat oven to 180°C/160°C fan-forced. Grease deep 26.5cm x 33cm (14-cup/3.5-litre) baking dish; line base with baking paper.
2 Combine the water, sugar, butter, sifted cocoa and soda in medium saucepan; stir over heat, without boiling, until sugar dissolves. Bring to the boil; reduce heat, simmer, uncovered, 5 minutes. Transfer mixture to large bowl; cool.
3 Add flour and egg to bowl; beat with an electric mixer until mixture is smooth and paler in colour. Pour mixture into dish. Bake about 50 minutes. Stand cake 10 minutes; turn, top-side up, onto wire rack to cool.
4 Meanwhile, make fudge frosting. Spread cold cake with fudge frosting.
fudge frosting Combine butter, the water and caster sugar in small saucepan; stir over heat, without boiling, until sugar dissolves. Sift icing sugar and cocoa powder into medium bowl; gradually stir in hot butter mixture. Cover; refrigerate about 20 minutes or until frosting thickens. Beat with wooden spoon until frosting is spreadable.

preparation time 20 minutes (plus cooling time)
cooking time 1 hour
serves 20
notes Choose a perfectly level-bottomed baking dish; one made from cast aluminium is the best choice, but almost any type will work. If the cake appears to be cooking too quickly in the corners of the dish, reduce the oven temperature to 160°C/140°C fan-forced; this will increase cooking time by up to 15 minutes.

gluten-free chocolate cake

You will need one large (230g) overripe banana for this recipe.

1 cup (125g) soy flour
¾ cup (110g) cornflour
(100% corn)
1¼ teaspoons bicarbonate
of soda
½ cup (50g) cocoa powder
1¼ cups (275g) caster sugar
150g butter, melted
1 tablespoon white vinegar
1 cup (250ml) evaporated milk
2 eggs
½ cup mashed banana
2 tablespoons raspberry jam
300ml thickened cream

1 Preheat oven to 180°C/160°C fan-forced. Grease two 22cm-round sandwich cake pans; line bases with baking paper.
2 Sift flours, soda, cocoa and sugar into large bowl; add butter, vinegar and milk. Beat with electric mixer on low speed 1 minute. Add eggs, banana and jam; beat on medium speed 2 minutes. Pour mixture into prepared pans.
3 Bake about 30 minutes. Stand cakes in pans 5 minutes; turn, top-side up, onto wire racks to cool.
4 Beat cream in small bowl with electric mixer until firm peaks form. Sandwich cakes with whipped cream; lightly dust with sifted icing sugar or sifted cocoa powder, if desired.

preparation time 20 minutes
(plus cooling time)
cooking time 30 minutes
serves 8
notes Cornflour comes in two types, wheaten and corn. Make sure you use 100% corn (maize) cornflour in this recipe.
Store unfilled cakes in airtight containers for up to two days. Sandwich cake with whipped cream close to serving. Cake is not suitable to freeze.

rich chocolate meringue cake

8 egg whites
1 cup (220g) caster sugar
60g dark cooking chocolate, chopped finely
¼ cup (60g) finely chopped glacé figs
¼ cup (45g) finely chopped seeded prunes
¾ cup (50g) stale breadcrumbs
¼ cup (25g) cocoa powder
1 tablespoon icing sugar
1 tablespoon cocoa powder, extra

1 Preheat oven to 120°C/100°C fan-forced. Grease 22cm springform tin; line base and side with baking paper.
2 Beat egg whites in medium bowl with electric mixer until soft peaks form. Add sugar, 1 tablespoon at a time, beating until sugar dissolves between each addition. Fold in chocolate, fruit, breadcrumbs and sifted cocoa.
3 Spoon mixture into prepared tin; bake 1½ hours. Cool in oven with door ajar.
4 Dust with combined sifted icing sugar and extra cocoa; serve with whipped cream, if desired.

preparation time 15 minutes (plus cooling time)
cooking time 1 hour 30 minutes
serves 8

triple chocolate brownies

125g butter, chopped
200g dark eating chocolate, chopped coarsely
½ cup (110g) caster sugar
2 eggs, beaten lightly
1¼ cups (185g) plain flour
150g white eating chocolate, chopped coarsely
100g milk eating chocolate, chopped coarsely

1 Preheat oven to 180°C/160°C fan-forced. Grease deep 19cm-square cake pan; line base and sides with baking paper.
2 Combine butter and dark chocolate in medium saucepan; stir over low heat until melted. Cool 10 minutes.
3 Stir sugar and egg into mixture. Stir in flour, then white and milk chocolates. Spread mixture into pan.
4 Bake about 35 minutes or until mixture is firm to touch. Cool in pan. If desired, sprinkle with sifted icing sugar before cutting.

preparation time 20 minutes (plus cooling time)
cooking time 35 minutes
serves 12
tip Brownies can be made three days ahead; store in an airtight container.

caramel and chocolate slice

½ cup (75g) plain flour
½ cup (75g) self-raising flour
1 cup (90g) rolled oats
¾ cup (165g) firmly packed brown sugar
150g butter, melted
125g dark eating chocolate, chopped coarsely
½ cup (55g) coarsely chopped walnuts
¼ cup (35g) plain flour, extra
½ cup (125ml) caramel topping

1 Preheat oven to 180°C/160°C fan-forced. Grease 19cm x 29cm rectangular slice pan; line base and two long sides with baking paper, extending paper 5cm above edges.
2 Combine flours, oats and sugar in medium bowl; stir in butter. Press half the mixture into pan. Bake 10 minutes. Remove from oven, sprinkle with chocolate and walnuts.
3 Blend extra flour with caramel topping in small bowl. Drizzle evenly over chocolate and walnuts, then sprinkle with remaining oat mixture.
4 Bake further 15 minutes. Cool in pan before cutting into squares to serve.

preparation time 20 minutes (plus cooling time)
cooking time 25 minutes
serves 15
tips We used a thick, caramel-flavoured ice-cream topping in this recipe.

chewy choc-chunk cookies

2 eggs

1⅓ cups (295g) firmly packed brown sugar

1 teaspoon vanilla extract

1 cup (150g) plain flour

¾ cup (110g) self-raising flour

½ teaspoon bicarbonate of soda

½ cup (125ml) vegetable oil

1 cup (120g) coarsely chopped roasted pecans

¾ cup (120g) coarsely chopped raisins

1 cup (150g) dark chocolate Melts, halved

½ cup (95g) white choc Bits

1 Preheat oven to 200°C/180°C fan-forced. Grease three oven trays.

2 Beat eggs, sugar and extract in small bowl with electric mixer about 1 minute or until mixture becomes lighter in colour.

3 Stir in sifted dry ingredients then remaining ingredients (the mixture will be soft). Cover bowl; refrigerate 1 hour.

4 Roll heaped tablespoons of the mixture into balls; place onto trays about 6cm apart, flatten into 6cm rounds.

5 Bake about 10 minutes or until browned lightly. Stand cookies on trays 5 minutes then transfer to a wire rack to cool.

preparation time 25 minutes (plus refrigeration and cooling time)

cooking time 10 minutes per tray

makes 20

notes Walnuts can be substituted for pecans, if desired. Cookies can be made up to one week ahead; store in an airtight container.

fudgy-wudgy chocolate cookies

125g butter, chopped
1 teaspoon vanilla extract
1¼ cups (275g) firmly packed brown sugar
1 egg
1 cup (150g) plain flour
¼ cup (35g) self-raising flour
1 teaspoon bicarbonate of soda
⅓ cup (35g) cocoa powder
½ cup (75g) raisins
¾ cup (110g) unsalted macadamia nuts, roasted, chopped coarsely
½ cup (95g) dark choc Bits
½ cup (75g) dark chocolate Melts, halved

1 Preheat oven to 180°C/160°C fan-forced. Line three oven trays
with baking paper.
2 Beat butter, extract, sugar and egg in medium bowl with electric mixer
until smooth. Stir in sifted flours, soda and cocoa powder; stir in raisins,
nuts and both chocolates.
3 Drop rounded tablespoons of mixture onto trays about 4cm apart;
press each with hand to flatten slightly.
4 Bake 10 minutes. Stand cookies on trays 5 minutes then transfer to
a wire rack to cool.

preparation time 15 minutes (plus cooling time)
cooking time 10 minutes
makes 24
notes Other nuts, such as walnuts or pecans, can be used instead
of macadamias. Cookies can be made up to one week ahead; store
in an airtight container.

nanaimo bars

Named after the city of Nanaimo, British Columbia, the nanaimo bar originated in Canada, but is also popular across North America. A type of no-bake chocolate slice, it consists of a crumb-based layer, topped by a layer of light custard or vanilla butter icing, which is covered in soft chocolate.

185g butter, chopped
100g dark eating chocolate, coarsely chopped
1 egg
2 cups (200g) wheatmeal biscuit crumbs
1 cup (80g) desiccated coconut
⅔ cup (80g) finely chopped pecans
custard filling
60g butter, softened
1 teaspoon vanilla extract
2 cups (320g) icing sugar
2 tablespoons custard powder
¼ cup (60ml) milk
chocolate topping
30g dark eating chocolate
15g butter

1 Grease 19cm x 29cm rectangular slice pan; line base and two long sides with baking paper, extending paper 5cm above edges.
2 Make custard filling.
3 Melt butter and chocolate in large bowl over hot water until smooth; stir in egg.
4 Add biscuit crumbs, coconut and nuts; mix well. Press mixture firmly over base of pan. Spread evenly with filling. Refrigerate until firm.
5 Make chocolate topping.
6 Drizzle slice with topping; refrigerate 3 hours or overnight until topping is set. Cut into pieces before serving.

custard filling Beat butter and extract in small bowl with electric mixer until as white as possible; gradually beat in sifted icing sugar and custard powder, then milk.

chocolate topping Melt chocolate and butter in small bowl over hot water.

preparation time 45 minutes
(plus refrigeration time)
serves 16
notes Recipe can be made up to two weeks ahead; store, covered, in the refrigerator. The butter and chocolate for the base and topping can be melted together in a microwave oven.

chocolate nut slice

½ x 395g can sweetened condensed milk
250g dark eating chocolate, melted
½ cup (70g) coarsely chopped roasted hazelnuts
½ cup (60g) coarsely chopped roasted pecans
½ cup (80g) coarsely chopped roasted blanched almonds

1 Grease 8cm x 26cm bar cake pan; line base and sides with baking paper, extending paper 5cm above long sides.
2 Combine ingredients in medium bowl. Spread mixture into pan.
3 Refrigerate several hours or overnight until firm.

preparation time 15 minutes (plus refrigeration time)
serves 18
notes Any combination of nuts can be used. Slice can be kept, wrapped in plastic wrap and refrigerated, for up to four weeks.

white chocolate and pistachio parfait

¾ cup (180ml) thickened
cream
250g white eating chocolate,
chopped coarsely
6 egg yolks
2 eggs
½ cup (110g) caster sugar
1⅔ cups (410ml) thickened
cream, extra
½ cup (125ml) irish cream
liqueur
1 cup (140g) pistachios,
roasted, chopped finely
berry compote
300g frozen mixed berries
2 tablespoons caster sugar
1 tablespoon water

1 Combine cream and chocolate in medium saucepan; stir over low heat until smooth.

2 Beat yolks, eggs and sugar in small bowl with electric mixer until thick and creamy; with motor operating, gradually beat hot chocolate mixture into egg mixture. Transfer parfait mixture to large bowl, cover; refrigerate about 30 minutes or until mixture thickens slightly.

3 Meanwhile, cut eight 30cm squares of baking paper; fold one square in half diagonally. Hold the apex of the triangle towards you, and roll the paper into a cone shape by bringing the three points of the triangle together. Staple the bag together just below where the three points meet to hold its shape; stand cone upright in tall glass. Repeat with remaining paper squares, standing each in a tall glass; place glasses on tray.

4 Beat extra cream in small bowl with electric mixer until soft peaks form; fold cream, liqueur and nuts into parfait mixture. Divide mixture among cones. Cover cones loosely with plastic wrap; freeze overnight.

5 Make berry compote.

6 Turn parfaits onto individual serving plates; carefully remove and discard paper from each. Serve with berry compote.

berry compote Combine ingredients in small saucepan; stir over low heat until sugar dissolves. Cool 10 minutes.

preparation time 30 minutes
(plus refrigeration and freezing time)
cooking time 10 minutes
serves 8

chocolate hazelnut ice-cream

2 litres (8 cups) vanilla ice-cream
¾ cup (180ml) chocolate-hazelnut spread, warmed
½ cup (60g) finely chopped roasted hazelnuts
1 tablespoon coffee-flavoured liqueur
2 teaspoons dry instant coffee

1 Line base of 14cm x 21cm loaf pan with strip of baking paper, extending paper over two opposite sides.
2 Divide ice-cream into two equal portions; return one portion to freezer.
3 Beat softened ice-cream with chocolate-hazelnut spread in small bowl with electric mixer until smooth; stir in nuts. Pour mixture into prepared pan, cover; freeze until firm.
4 Combine liqueur and coffee in small bowl; stir until coffee is dissolved. Beat remaining softened ice-cream in small bowl with electric mixer until smooth; stir in liqueur mixture. Pour over ice-cream in pan, cover; freeze until firm. Turn ice-cream onto board, remove paper; cut in slices to serve. Serve with mixed berries, fresh mint and chocolate curls, if you like.

preparation time 25 minutes (plus freezing time)
serves 6

chocolate cookie ice-cream

2 litres (8 cups) vanilla ice-cream, softened
200g Penguin biscuits, chopped coarsely
100g dark eating chocolate, chopped finely
6 ice-cream cones
chocolate topping
100g dark eating chocolate, chopped coarsely
1 teaspoon vegetable oil

1 Beat ice-cream in large bowl with electric mixer until smooth; stir in biscuits and chocolate. Pour into loaf pan, cover; freeze until firm.
2 Make chocolate topping.
3 Scoop ice-cream into cones; drizzle with chocolate topping.
chocolate topping Melt chocolate and oil in small bowl over hot water.

preparation time 10 minutes (plus freezing time)
cooking time 5 minutes
serves 6
tip The chocolate and oil for the topping can be melted together in a microwave oven. Make topping just before serving ice-cream.

white chocolate and strawberry bombe

½ cup (110g) caster sugar
2 tablespoons instant coffee granules
1½ cups (375ml) water
250g packet sponge finger biscuits
3 eggs, separated
1 cup (250g) mascarpone cheese
½ cup (110g) caster sugar, extra
½ cup (125ml) thickened cream
125g white eating chocolate, chopped finely
375g strawberries, sliced

1 Combine sugar, coffee and the water in small saucepan; stir over low heat, without boiling, until sugar is dissolved.
2 Immerse three-quarters of the biscuits, one at a time, in coffee mixture, then arrange them, in a single layer, over base and side of a 2-litre (8-cup) aluminium pudding steamer.
3 Beat egg whites in small bowl with electric mixer until firm peaks form. Beat egg yolks, cheese, extra sugar and cream in medium bowl with electric mixer until smooth; fold in egg whites and chocolate.
4 Spread half the cream mixture over biscuits in steamer, top with half the strawberries; repeat layers.
5 Dip remaining biscuits in remaining coffee mixture; arrange over top of strawberries. Cover; freeze until firm. Turn onto plate about 10 minutes before serving.

preparation time 25 minutes (plus freezing time)
serves 8 to 10

gourmet chocolate tart

2 eggs
2 egg yolks
¼ cup (55g) caster sugar
250g dark eating chocolate, melted
200g butter, melted
tart shell
1½ cups (225g) plain flour
½ cup (110g) caster sugar
140g cold butter, chopped
1 egg, beaten lightly

1 Make tart shell.

2 Reduce oven temperature to 180°C/160°C fan-forced.

3 Whisk eggs, egg yolks and sugar in medium heatproof bowl over medium saucepan of simmering water about 15 minutes or until light and fluffy. Gently whisk chocolate and butter into egg mixture.

4 Pour mixture into tart shell. Bake, uncovered, about 10 minutes or until filling is set; cool 10 minutes. Refrigerate 1 hour. Serve dusted with sifted cocoa powder, if desired.

tart shell Blend or process flour, sugar and butter until crumbly; add egg, process until ingredients just come together. Knead dough on floured surface until smooth. Enclose in plastic wrap; refrigerate 30 minutes. Grease 24cm-round loose-based flan tin. Roll dough between sheets of baking paper until large enough to line tin. Lift dough into tin, press into side; trim edge, prick base all over with fork. Cover; refrigerate 30 minutes. Preheat oven to 200°C/180°C fan-forced. Place tin on oven tray; cover dough with baking paper, fill with dried beans or rice. Bake, uncovered, 10 minutes. Remove paper and beans carefully from tin; bake, uncovered, about 5 minutes or until tart shell browns lightly. Cool to room temperature.

preparation time 30 minutes (plus refrigeration time)
cooking time 40 minutes
serves 8

chocolate roulade

200g dark cooking chocolate,
  chopped coarsely
¼ cup (60ml) hot water
1 tablespoon instant coffee
  granules
4 eggs, separated
½ cup (110g) caster sugar
1 tablespoon caster sugar,
  extra
1 teaspoon hot water, extra
300ml whipping cream
2 tablespoons coffee-
  flavoured liqueur
1 tablespoon icing sugar

1 Preheat oven to 180°C/160°C fan-forced. Grease 25cm x 30cm swiss roll pan; line base with baking paper.

2 Combine chocolate, the water and half the coffee granules in large heatproof bowl. Stir over large saucepan of simmering water until smooth; remove from heat.

3 Beat egg yolks and caster sugar in small bowl with electric mixer until thick and creamy; fold egg mixture into warm chocolate mixture.

4 Meanwhile, beat egg whites in clean small bowl with electric mixer until soft peaks form; fold egg whites, in two batches, into chocolate mixture. Spread into prepared pan; bake in oven about 10 minutes.

5 Place a piece of baking paper cut a little larger then the swiss roll pan on bench; sprinkle evenly with extra caster sugar. Turn cake onto sugared paper, peel lining paper away; use serrated knife to cut away crisp edges from all sides. Cover cake with tea towel; cool.

6 Dissolve remaining coffee granules in the extra water in small bowl. Add cream, liqueur and sifted icing sugar; beat with electric mixer until firm peaks form. Spread cake evenly with cream mixture. Roll cake, from long side, by lifting paper and using it to guide the roll into shape. Cover roll; refrigerate 30 minutes before serving.

preparation time 20 minutes
(plus refrigeration time)
cooking time 10 minutes
serves 8

black forest gateau

250g butter
1 tablespoon instant coffee granules
1½ cups (375ml) hot water
200g dark eating chocolate, chopped coarsely
2 cups (440g) caster sugar
1½ cups (225g) self-raising flour
1 cup (150g) plain flour
¼ cup (25g) cocoa powder
2 eggs
2 teaspoons vanilla extract
600ml whipping cream
¼ cup (60ml) kirsch
2 x 425g cans cherries, drained, seeded

1 Preheat oven to 150°C/130°C fan-forced. Grease deep 23cm-round cake pan, line base and side with baking paper; grease paper well.
2 Melt butter in medium saucepan, stir in combined coffee and hot water, then chocolate and sugar; stir over low heat, without boiling, until smooth. Transfer to large bowl, cool until warm.
3 Beat mixture on low speed with electric mixer; gradually beat in sifted dry ingredients, in three batches. Beat in eggs, one at a time, then extract. Pour into prepared pan. Bake in oven about 1¾ hours. Stand in pan 5 minutes; turn, top-side up, onto wire rack to cool.
4 Beat cream until firm peaks form. Trim top of cake to make it flat. Split cake into three layers. Place one layer on serving plate, brush with one-third of the kirsch, top with one-third of the cream and half of the cherries. Repeat layering once more, then top with cake top. Brush top of cake with remaining kirsch; spread with remaining cream. Decorate the cake with fresh cherries and chocolate shavings, if desired.

preparation time 35 minutes (plus cooling time)
cooking time 1 hour 50 minutes
serves 12
tip Cake will keep for up to three days, covered, in the refrigerator.

chocolate mocha terrine

4 egg whites
1 cup (220g) caster sugar
2 tablespoons cocoa powder
200g dark eating chocolate, chopped coarsely
¾ cup (180ml) cream
2 teaspoons cocoa powder, extra

mocha butter cream
1 tablespoon instant coffee granules
2 tablespoons boiling water
100g unsalted butter, softened
2¼ cups (360g) icing sugar

1 Preheat oven to 150°C/130°C fan-forced. Line three oven trays with baking paper; draw a 10cm x 25cm rectangle on each piece.
2 Beat egg whites in medium bowl with electric mixer until soft peaks form. Gradually add sugar, beating after each addition until sugar dissolves; fold in sifted cocoa.
3 Spread meringue mixture evenly over drawn rectangles; bake, uncovered, about 45 minutes or until meringue is dry. Turn off oven; cool meringues in oven with door ajar.
4 Meanwhile, stir chocolate and cream in small saucepan over low heat until smooth, transfer to small bowl; refrigerate until firm. Beat chocolate mixture with electric mixer about 20 seconds or until just changed in colour.
5 Make mocha butter cream.
6 Place one meringue layer on serving plate; spread with half the chocolate mixture, then top with half the butter cream. Top with another meringue layer; spread with remaining chocolate mixture, then remaining butter cream. Top with last meringue layer, cover; refrigerate 3 hours or overnight. To serve, dust with sifted extra cocoa powder.

mocha butter cream Dissolve coffee with the water in small bowl; cool 10 minutes. Beat butter in small bowl with electric mixer until pale in colour; gradually add sifted icing sugar, beating until combined. Beat in coffee mixture.

preparation time 20 minutes
(plus cooling and refrigeration time)
cooking time 50 minutes
serves 12

chocolate irish cream mousse

6 eggs, separated
½ cup (80g) icing sugar
¼ cup (25g) cocoa powder
2 tablespoons cornflour
150g dark eating chocolate,
  melted
1 tablespoon water
600ml cream
450g dark eating chocolate,
  chopped coarsely, extra
¾ cup (180ml) irish cream
  liqueur
1 tablespoon cocoa powder,
  extra

1 Preheat oven to 180°C/160°C fan-forced. Grease 25cm x 30cm swiss roll pan; line base and sides with baking paper.

2 Beat egg yolks and sifted icing sugar in small bowl with electric mixer until thick and creamy; transfer to large bowl. Fold in sifted cocoa and cornflour, then chocolate; fold in the water.

3 Beat egg whites in medium bowl with electric mixer until soft peaks form. Fold egg whites, in two batches, into chocolate mixture. Spread mixture into prepared pan; bake about 15 minutes. Turn cake onto baking-paper-covered wire rack. Cover cake with baking paper; cool to room temperature.

4 Grease 22cm springform tin; line side with baking paper, bringing paper 5cm above edge. Cut 22cm-diameter circle from cooled cake; place in prepared tin. Discard remaining cake.

5 Combine cream and extra chocolate in medium saucepan; stir over low heat until smooth. Transfer to large bowl; refrigerate until just cold.

6 Add liqueur to chocolate mixture; beat with electric mixer until mixture changes to a paler colour. Pour mixture into prepared tin; refrigerate about 3 hours or until set.

7 Transfer cake from tin to serving plate; dust with sifted extra cocoa.

preparation time 30 minutes
(plus cooling and refrigeration time)
cooking time 15 minutes
serves 12
tip Do not overbeat the chocolate and liqueur mixture as it will curdle.

dark chocolate and almond torte

160g dark eating chocolate,
chopped coarsely
160g unsalted butter,
chopped
5 eggs, separated
¾ cup (165g) caster sugar
1 cup (120g) almond meal
⅔ cup (50g) toasted flaked
almonds, chopped coarsely
⅓ cup (35g) coarsely grated
dark eating chocolate
1 cup (150g) vienna almonds
dark chocolate ganache
125g dark eating chocolate,
chopped coarsely
⅓ cup (80ml) thickened cream

1 Preheat oven to 180°C/160°C fan-forced.
Grease deep 22cm-round cake pan; line base
and side with two layers of baking paper.
2 Stir chopped chocolate and butter in small
saucepan over low heat until smooth; cool to
room temperature.
3 Beat egg yolks and sugar in small bowl with
electric mixer until thick and creamy. Transfer to
large bowl; fold in chocolate mixture, almond
meal, flaked almonds and grated chocolate.
4 Beat egg whites in small bowl with electric
mixer until soft peaks form; fold into chocolate
mixture, in two batches. Pour mixture into pan;
bake, uncovered, in oven about 45 minutes.
Stand cake in pan 15 minutes; turn cake,
top-side up, onto wire rack to cool.
5 Meanwhile, make dark chocolate ganache.
6 Spread ganache over top of cake, decorate
cake with vienna almonds; stand 30 minutes
before serving.

dark chocolate ganache Stir ingredients in
small saucepan over low heat until smooth.

preparation time 20 minutes
(plus cooling and standing time)
cooking time 55 minutes
serves 14
note Vienna (candied) almonds are whole
almonds coated in toffee; they're available from
selected supermarkets, nut shops and gourmet
food and specialty confectionery stores.

white chocolate and lemon lime truffles

½ cup (125ml) coconut cream
2 teaspoons finely grated lime rind
2 teaspoons finely grated lemon rind
360g white eating chocolate, chopped coarsely
1¼ cups (85g) shredded coconut

1 Combine coconut cream, rinds and chocolate in small saucepan; stir over low heat until smooth. Transfer mixture to small bowl, cover; refrigerate 3 hours or overnight.
2 Working with a quarter of the mixture at a time (keeping remainder under refrigeration), roll rounded teaspoons into balls; place on tray. Refrigerate truffles until firm.
3 Working quickly, roll truffles in coconut, return to tray; refrigerate until firm.

preparation time 40 minutes (plus refrigeration time)
cooking time 5 minutes
makes 30

dark chocolate, cranberry, and port truffles

¼ cup (60ml) thickened cream
200g dark eating chocolate, chopped coarsely
2 tablespoons port
⅓ cup (45g) dried cranberries, chopped coarsely
300g dark eating chocolate, melted

1 Combine cream and chopped chocolate in small saucepan; stir over low heat until smooth, stir in port and cranberries. Transfer to small bowl, cover; refrigerate 3 hours or overnight.
2 Working with a quarter of the mixture at a time (keeping remainder under refrigeration), roll rounded teaspoons into balls; place on tray. Freeze truffles until firm.
3 Working quickly, dip truffles in melted chocolate then roll gently in hands to coat evenly, return to tray; refrigerate until firm.

preparation time 40 minutes (plus refrigeration and freezing time)
cooking time 5 minutes
makes 30

dark chocolate and ginger truffles

⅓ cup (80ml) thickened cream
200g dark eating chocolate, chopped coarsely
½ cup (115g) glacé ginger, chopped finely
¼ cup (25g) cocoa powder

1   Combine cream and chocolate in small saucepan; stir over
low heat until smooth, stir in ginger. Transfer to small bowl, cover;
refrigerate 3 hours or overnight.
2   Working with a quarter of the mixture at a time (keeping remainder
under refrigeration), roll rounded teaspoons into balls; place on tray.
Refrigerate truffles until firm.
3   Working quickly, roll balls in cocoa, return to tray; refrigerate truffles
until firm.

preparation time 40 minutes (plus refrigeration time)
cooking time 5 minutes
makes 30

chocolate and peanut butter truffles

⅓ cup (80ml) thickened cream
200g milk eating chocolate, chopped coarsely
¼ cup (70g) unsalted crunchy peanut butter
¾ cup (110g) crushed peanuts

1 Combine cream and chocolate in small saucepan; stir over low heat
until smooth, stir in peanut butter. Transfer to small bowl, cover; refrigerate
3 hours or overnight.
2 Working with a quarter of the mixture at a time (keeping remainder
under refrigeration), roll rounded teaspoons into balls; place on tray.
Refrigerate truffles until firm.
3 Working quickly, roll balls in peanuts, return to tray; refrigerate truffles
until firm.

preparation time 40 minutes (plus refrigeration time)
cooking time 5 minutes
makes 30

chocolate nut tree

Bring out this tree with the coffee, suggesting to your guests that they snap off bits of the branches. Or, for an impressive gift, wrap the whole tree in cellophane and deliver it on the day.

24cm-round covered cake board
500g dark eating chocolate, melted
1 cup (140g) toasted slivered almonds, chopped finely
½ cup (110g) finely chopped dried figs
100g dark eating chocolate, melted, extra
1 brazil nut
2 teaspoons icing sugar

1 Grease four oven trays; line each with baking paper. Mark nine crosses, measuring 7cm, 9cm, 11cm, 13cm, 14cm, 15cm, 16cm, 17cm and 18cm on trays, leaving about 3cm space between each cross. Mark an 18cm cross on cake board.

2 Combine chocolate, almonds and figs in medium bowl. Drop teaspoonfuls of the chocolate mixture along all the marked crosses on paper to make branches; refrigerate several hours or overnight.

3 Drop about a teaspoon of the extra melted chocolate onto the centre of the 18cm cross on cake board; position the 18cm branch on top, moving it around until the best position is found.

4 Assemble the remaining eight branches in pairs, starting from the largest branch and finishing with the smallest, using about a teaspoon of the extra melted chocolate in the centre of each crossed pair; refrigerate until set.

5 Secure each pair to the next with a little melted chocolate (if the branches look a little uneven, support them underneath with a match box). Secure brazil nut to centre of smallest branch with remaining melted chocolate; refrigerate until chocolate sets between branches. Store tree in refrigerator until required; dust with sifted icing sugar before serving.

preparation time 30 minutes
(plus refrigeration time)
serves 8

glossary

almonds flat pointy-tipped nuts having a pitted brown shell enclosing a creamy white kernel that is covered by a brown skin.
  blanched skins removed.
  flaked paper-thin slices.
  meal also known as ground almonds; nuts are powdered to a coarse flour texture. Used in baking or as a thickening agent.
  slivered small pieces cut lengthways.
  vienna toffee-coated.
bicarbonate of soda also known as baking soda or carb soda.
biscuits also known as cookies.
  amaretti baked biscuits made of sugar, egg whites, and almond meal.
  wheatmeal has a crunchy, yet soft, buttery texture, that can be crushed into fine or coarse crumbs. Digestive biscuits may also be used.
brazil nut a triangular nut with a hard shell and a white flesh encased with a brown skin.
breadcrumbs, stale one- or two-day-old bread made into crumbs by grating, blending or processing.
butter use salted or unsalted (sweet) butter; 125g is equal to one stick of butter.
chocolate
  bittersweet we use dark eating chocolate; made of cocoa liquor, cocoa butter and sugar.

choc Bits also known as chocolate morsels and chocolate chips; available in milk, white and dark chocolate. Made of cocoa liquor, cocoa butter, sugar and an emulsifier; these hold their shape in baking and are ideal for decorating.
couverture a fine quality, very rich chocolate high in both cocoa butter and cocoa liquor.
dark eating also known as semi-sweet or luxury chocolate; made of cocoa liquor and cocoa butter and a little sugar.
chocolate-hazelnut spread we use Nutella; originally developed when chocolate was in short supply during World War 2, so hazelnuts were added to stretch the chocolate supply.
Melts discs of compounded milk, white or dark chocolate ideal for melting as well as moulding and piping.
milk eating most popular eating chocolate; mild and very sweet.
white eating contains no cocoa solids but derives its sweet flavour from cocoa butter. Very sensitive to heat.
cinnamon dried inner bark of the shoots of the cinnamon tree; available in stick (quills) or ground form.
cocoa powder unsweetened, dried, roasted then ground cocoa beans.

coconut
  cream not the juice found inside the fruit, which is known as coconut water, but the first pressing of the coconut flesh alone, without the addition of water.
  desiccated unsweetened, concentrated, dried, finely shredded coconut.
  flaked the dried, flaked, flesh of the coconut.
  shredded thin strips of dried coconut.
coffee-flavoured liqueur we use Kahlúa.
cornflour also known as cornstarch; used as a thickening agent in cooking.
cranberries, dried have the same slightly sour, succulent flavour as fresh cranberries. Dried sweetened cranberries have the addition of a sweetener. Available in most supermarkets.
cream we use fresh cream, also known as pure cream and pouring cream, unless otherwise stated.
  thickened a whipping cream containing a thickener.
currants dried tiny, almost black, raisins.
custard powder packaged vanilla mixture used to make pouring custard.
dates fruit of the date palm tree, eaten fresh or dried. About 4-6cm in length, oval and plump, thin-skinned, with a honey-sweet flavour and sticky texture.

drambuie honey- and herb-flavoured scotch whisky.

evaporated milk canned, unsweetened milk from which water has been extracted by evaporation.

figs vary in skin and flesh colour according to type not ripeness. When ripe, figs should be unblemished and bursting with flesh; nectar beads at the base indicate when a fig is at its best.

flour

   plain an all-purpose flour made from wheat.

   self-raising plain flour sifted with baking powder in the proportion of 1 cup flour to 2 teaspoons baking powder.

   soy made from roasted soya beans ground into a fine powder.

glacé ginger fresh ginger root preserved in sugar syrup. Crystallised ginger can be substituted if rinsed with warm water and dried before using.

hazelnuts also known as filberts; plump, grape-size, rich, sweet nut having a brown inedible skin that is removed by rubbing heated nuts together vigorously in a tea towel.

   meal also known as ground hazelnuts.

irish cream liqueur we use Baileys, a smooth, creamy blend of fresh irish cream, spirits, whisky, cocoa and vanilla.

jam also known as preserve or conserve; most often made from fruit.

Kahlúa a coffee-flavoured liqueur.

kirsch cherry-flavoured liqueur.

macadamia a rich, buttery nut; store in refrigerator because of high oil content.

mascarpone cheese a buttery-rich, cream-like cheese made from cows milk. It is ivory-coloured, soft and delicate, with the texture of softened butter.

mixed peel candied citrus peel.

nutmeg the dried nut of an evergreen tree native to Indonesia; it is available in ground form or you can grate your own with a fine grater.

peanut butter peanuts that have been ground into a paste; available in crunchy or smooth varieties; also known as peanut paste.

pecan a golden-brown, rich, buttery nut.

pistachios pale green, delicately flavoured nut inside hard off-white shells. To peel, soak shelled nuts in boiling water for about 5 minutes; drain, then pat dry with absorbent paper. Rub skins with a cloth to peel.

port a fortified wine to which additional alcohol has been added, most commonly in the form of brandy.

prunes dried plums; store in the refrigerator.

raisins dried sweet grapes.

rolled oats oat groats (oats that have been husked) steamed-softened, flattened with rollers and dried.

sponge finger biscuits also known as Savoiardi, savoy biscuits, lady's fingers or sponge fingers; are Italian-style crisp fingers made from sponge-cake mixture.

sugar

   brown an extremely soft, finely granulated sugar retaining molasses for its colour and flavour.

   caster also known as finely granulated or superfine table sugar.

   icing sugar also known as confectioners' sugar or powdered sugar; granulated sugar crushed together with a small amount of cornflour.

   raw brown granulated sugar.

   white also known as crystal or granulated table sugar.

sultanas dried grapes, also known as golden raisins.

sweetened condensed milk milk from which 60% of the water has been removed; the remaining milk is then sweetened with sugar.

vanilla extract obtained from vanilla beans infused in water.

vegetable oil sourced from plants rather than animal fats.

white vinegar made from spirit of cane sugar.

conversion chart

MEASURES

One Australian metric measuring cup holds approximately 250ml, one Australian metric tablespoon holds 20ml, one Australian metric teaspoon holds 5ml.

The difference between one country's measuring cups and another's is within a 2- or 3-teaspoon variance, and will not affect your cooking results. North America, New Zealand and the United Kingdom use a 15ml tablespoon. All cup and spoon measurements are level. The most accurate way of measuring dry ingredients is to weigh them. When measuring liquids, use a clear glass or plastic jug with metric markings.

We use large eggs with an average weight of 60g.

DRY MEASURES

METRIC	IMPERIAL
15g	½oz
30g	1oz
60g	2oz
90g	3oz
125g	4oz (¼lb)
155g	5oz
185g	6oz
220g	7oz
250g	8oz (½lb)
280g	9oz
315g	10oz
345g	11oz
375g	12oz (¾lb)
410g	13oz
440g	14oz
470g	15oz
500g	16oz (1lb)
750g	24oz (1½lb)
1kg	32oz (2lb)

LIQUID MEASURES

METRIC	IMPERIAL
30ml	1 fluid oz
60ml	2 fluid oz
100ml	3 fluid oz
125ml	4 fluid oz
150ml	5 fluid oz (¼ pint/1 gill)
190ml	6 fluid oz
250ml	8 fluid oz
300ml	10 fluid oz (½ pint)
500ml	16 fluid oz
600ml	20 fluid oz (1 pint)
1000ml (1 litre)	1¾ pints

LENGTH MEASURES

METRIC	IMPERIAL
3mm	⅛in
6mm	¼in
1cm	½in
2cm	¾in
2.5cm	1in
5cm	2in
6cm	2½in
8cm	3in
10cm	4in
13cm	5in
15cm	6in
18cm	7in
20cm	8in
23cm	9in
25cm	10in
28cm	11in
30cm	12in (1ft)

OVEN TEMPERATURES

These oven temperatures are only a guide for conventional ovens.
For fan-forced ovens, check the manufacturer's manual.

	°C (CELSIUS)	°F (FAHRENHEIT)	GAS MARK
Very slow	120	250	½
Slow	150	275-300	1-2
Moderately slow	160	325	3
Moderate	180	350-375	4-5
Moderately hot	200	400	6
Hot	220	425-450	7-8
Very hot	240	475	9

index

Are you missing some of the world's favourite cookbooks?

The Australian Women's Weekly cookbooks are available from bookshops, cookshops, supermarkets and other stores all over the world. You can also buy direct from the publisher, using the order form below.

MINI SERIES £3.50 190x138MM 64 PAGES

TITLE	QTY	TITLE	QTY	TITLE	QTY
4 Fast Ingredients		Gluten-free Cooking		Potatoes	
4 Kids to Cook		Grills & Barbecues		Quick Desserts	
15-minute Feasts		Healthy Everyday Food 4 Kids		Roast	
50 Fast Chicken Fillets		Ice-creams & Sorbets		Salads	
50 Fast Desserts		Indian Cooking		Simple Slices	
Barbecue Chicken		Indonesian Favourite		Simply Seafood	
Biscuits, Brownies & Bisotti		Irish Favourites		Soup plus	
Bites		Italian Favourites		Spanish Favourites	
Bowl Food		Jams & Jellies		Stir-fries	
Burgers, Rösti & Fritters		Japanese Favourites		Stir-fry Favourites	
Cafe Cakes		Kebabs & Skewers		Summer Salads	
Cafe Food		Kids Party Food		Summer Seafood	
Casseroles & Curries		Lebanese Cooking		Tagines & Couscous	
Char-grills & Barbecues		Low-Fat Delicious		Tapas, Antipasto & Mezze	
Cheesecakes, Pavlova & Trifles		Low Fat Fast		Tarts	
Chinese Favourites		Malaysian Favourites		Tex-Mex	
Chocolate Cakes		Mince Favourites		Thai Favourites	
Chocolate Favourites		Microwave		The Christmas Table	
Crumbles & Bakes		Muffins		The Fast Egg	
Cupcakes & Cookies		Noodles & Stir-fries		The Young Chef	
Dips & Dippers		Old-Fashioned Desserts		Vegetarian	
Dried Fruit & Nuts		Outdoor Eating		Vegie Main Meals	
Drinks		Packed Lunch		Vietnamese Favourites	
Easy Pies & Pastries		Party Food		Wok	
Fast Fillets		Pickles and Chutneys			
Fishcakes & Crispybakes		Pasta		TOTAL COST £	

Photocopy and complete coupon below

Name _____

Address _____

_____ Postcode _____

Country _____ Phone (business hours) _____

Email*(optional) _____

* By including your email address, you consent to receipt of any email regarding this magazine, and other emails which inform you of ACP's other publications, products, services and events, and to promote third party goods and services you may be interested in.

I enclose my cheque/money order for £ _____ or please charge £ _____ to my:

☐ Access ☐ Mastercard ☐ Visa ☐ Diners Club

Card number | | | | | | | | | | | | | | | |

3 digit security code *(found on reverse of card)* _____

Cardholder's signature _____ Expiry date ____ /____

To order: Mail or fax – photocopy or complete the order form above, and send your credit card details or cheque payable to: Australian Consolidated Press (UK), 10 Scirocco Close, Moulton Park Office Village, Northampton NN3 6AP, phone (+44) (01) 604 642200, fax (+44) (01) 604 642300, e-mail books@acpuk.com or order online at www.acpuk.com
Non-UK residents: We accept the credit cards listed on the coupon, or cheques, drafts or International Money Orders payable in sterling and drawn on a UK bank. Credit card charges are at the exchange rate current at the time of payment. All pricing current at time of going to press and subject to change/availability.
Postage and packing UK: Add £1.00 per order plus 75p per book.
Postage and packing overseas: Add £2.00 per order plus £1.50 per book. **Offer ends 31.12.2009**